Celebrating

CHICAGO BLACKHAWKS

The Original 6

Eric Zweig

Crabtree Publishing Company

www.crabtreebooks.com

Celebrating Hockey's History

The Original 6

Author: Eric Zweig,
  Member of the Society for International
  Hockey Research

Editor: Ellen Rodger

Editorial director: Kathy Middleton

Design: Tammy McGarr

Photo research: Tammy McGarr

Proofreader: Wendy Scavuzzo

**Production coordinator and
  Prepress technician:** Tammy McGarr

Print coordinator: Margaret Amy Salter

Photo Credits:
AP Images: p 5 (bottom)
Creative Commons: p 29 (top)
Getty Images: B Bennett, p 17 (bottom left)
Hockey Gods: pp 6,
Hockey Hall of Fame: Le Studio du Hockey, pp 7, 14, 21;
  Lewis Portnoy, p 10; Frank Prazak, p 11; Turofsky, p 12;
  Paul Bereswill, p 13 (middle right); Michael Sr. Burns, p 13
  (bottom left); Phil Pritchard, p 19;
Icon Sportswire: Marc Sanchez, p 18
Keystone: © Mike Wulf, front cover, title page, pp 24, 25, 27
Library of Congress: George Granthan Bain, p 28 (top);
Shutterstock: © Matthew Dicker, p 29 (bottom);
Wikimedia: Lisa Gansky, p 4; Ralston-Purina Company, makers
  of Chex cereals, pp 5 (top) 23 (top left and middle);
  Alex Goykhman, p 8; public domain, p 13 (top left);
  Charles Bird King (1785-1862), p 16; p 20; David Kindler, p 22;
  Conrad Poirier (1912-1968), p 23 (top right); Kelzeegla, p 26;
  p 28 (bottom)

Library and Archives Canada Cataloguing in Publication

Zweig, Eric, 1963-, author
        Chicago Blackhawks / Eric Zweig.

(The original six : celebrating hockey's history)
Includes index.
Issued in print and electronic formats.
ISBN 978-0-7787-3427-7 (hardcover).--
ISBN 978-0-7787-3443-7 (softcover).--
ISBN 978-1-4271-1922-3 (HTML)

        1. Chicago Blackhawks (Hockey team)--Juvenile literature.
2. Chicago Blackhawks (Hockey team)--History--Juvenile literature.
I. Title.

GV848.C48Z84 2017   j796.962'640977311   C2017-903477-4
                                                    C2017-903478-2

Library of Congress Cataloging-in-Publication Data

Names: Zweig, Eric, 1963- author.
Title: Chicago Blackhawks / Eric Zweig.
Description: New York : Crabtree Publishing Company, [2018] |
  Series: The Original Six: Celebrating hockey's history | Includes index.
  | Audience: Ages: 10-14. | Audience: Grades: 7 to 8.
Identifiers: LCCN 2017029651 (print) | LCCN 2017034424 (ebook) |
  ISBN 9781427119223 (Electronic HTML) |
  ISBN 9780778734277 (Reinforced library binding) |
  ISBN 9780778734437 (Paperback)
Subjects: LCSH: Chicago Blackhawks (Hockey team)--History--Juvenile
  literature. | National Hockey League--History--Juvenile literature. |
  Hockey--History--Juvenile literature.
Classification: LCC GV848.C48 (ebook) |
  LCC GV848.C48 Z94 2018 (print) | DDC 796.962/64077311--dc23
LC record available at https://lccn.loc.gov/2017029651

Crabtree Publishing Company

www.crabtreebooks.com   1-800-387-7650

Printed in the USA/102017/CG20170907

Published in Canada
Crabtree Publishing
616 Welland Ave.
St. Catharines, Ontario
L2M 5V6

Published in the United States
Crabtree Publishing
PMB 59051
350 Fifth Avenue, 59th Floor
New York, New York 10118

Published in the United Kingdom
Crabtree Publishing
Maritime House
Basin Road North, Hove
BN41 1WR

Published in Australia
Crabtree Publishing
3 Charles Street
Coburg North
VIC, 3058

Table of Contents

Winners in the Windy City	4
The NHL at 100	6
The Stanley Cup	8
Blackhawks' Best	10
Great Goalies	12
Blackhawks by the Numbers	14
Black, White, and Red	16
Trophy Winners	18
Behind the Bench	20
Blackhawks Bits and Pieces	22
Team Rivalries	24
Fan Frenzy	26
On Home Ice	28
Glossary, Further Reading, and Websites to Check Out	30
Test Your Blackhawks' Knowledge, Places to Go, and About the Author	31
Index	32

Celebrating Hockey's History

The Original 6

WINNERS IN THE WINDY CITY

Since winning the Stanley Cup in 2010, the Chicago Blackhawks have been the best team in the NHL. They don't win the cup every year, but they're always in contention, and they boast some of the biggest stars in the game today.

49-Year Drought

The Blackhawks were in big trouble back in 2007. Since 1997–98, they'd missed the playoffs eight times in nine seasons. Attendance was terrible. It was even hard to find the team's games on TV beyond the Chicago area. Still, there was hope on the horizon. Chicago had selected Jonathan Toews third overall in the 2006 NHL Draft. They got Patrick Kane with the #1 pick in 2007. Toews and Kane both made the team in 2007–08, and two years later, Chicago won the Stanley Cup. It was the first time the Blackhawks had won the cup in 49 years!

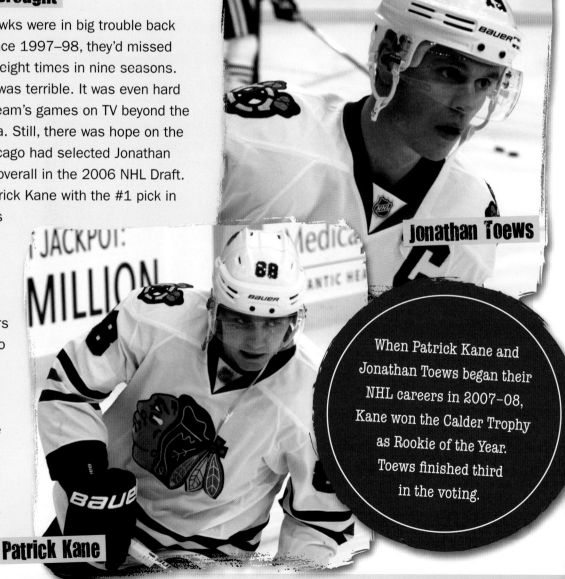

Jonathan Toews

Patrick Kane

When Patrick Kane and Jonathan Toews began their NHL careers in 2007–08, Kane won the Calder Trophy as Rookie of the Year. Toews finished third in the voting.

Building a Dynasty

It's hard to build a **dynasty** in modern sports. Teams used to be able to keep all the players they wanted until they decided to trade them. Now, **free agency** means players can leave their teams and sell their services to the highest bidder. NHL teams also have to deal with a salary cap that sets out how much they can pay for players. If you pay too much to your top stars, there won't be enough money left to put together a winning team. Chicago has managed to hold onto both Toews and Kane, as well as Duncan Keith, Brent Seabrook, and Marian Hossa, and still put together a solid roster of supporting players   year after year.

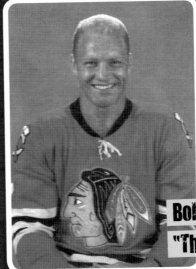

Bobby Hull was a rookie with Chicago in 1957-58. He finished second to Toronto Maple Leaf Frank Mahovlich in Calder Trophy voting that year.

Bobby Hull "The Golden Jet"

The Glory Years

The Blackhawks had been through similar struggles in the 1940s and 1950s. Chicago missed the playoffs 11 times in 12 seasons from 1946 to 1958. Back then, the team was rescued by new young stars Bobby Hull, Stan Mikita, and Pierre Pilote. Chicago won the Stanley Cup in 1961, and remained a top team into the early 1990s, although they wouldn't win the cup again until 2010.

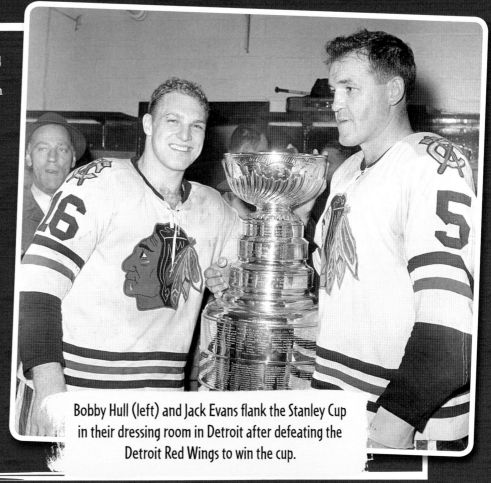

Bobby Hull (left) and Jack Evans flank the Stanley Cup in their dressing room in Detroit after defeating the Detroit Red Wings to win the cup.

THE NHL AT 100

The NHL has grown from three teams in its first season to 31 teams today. Chicago joined the NHL during the 1920s when the league grew to 10 teams. It became part of what is known as The Original Six with the Toronto Maple Leafs, Montreal Canadiens, Boston Bruins, Detroit Red Wings, and New York Rangers from 1942 until 1967.

Black Hawks to Blackhawks

The original owners of Chicago's new NHL team spent $100,000 to buy the Portland Rosebuds of the Western Hockey League (WHL) in May 1926. Major Frederic McLaughlin was the man in charge when Chicago officially joined the NHL on September 25, 1926. He named the team the Blackhawks after the United States Army's 86th Infantry "Blackhawk" Division, which he had served with during World War I. The team name, however, was usually spelled as two words—Black Hawks—until the 1985–86 season.

Proudly American

Chicago reached the Stanley Cup Finals in 1931 and won the cup for the first time in 1934. Major McLaughlin was a patriotic American and wanted as many American players as he could get on the Blackhawks. At a time when most NHL teams had only Canadian players, Chicago won the Stanley Cup again in 1938 with an American coach and eight Americans on the roster. No Stanley Cup winner would have more American players until the New Jersey Devils won with 12 in 1995.

Stanley Cup Trophy, 1934

Major Frederic McLaughlin

6

Norris Years

Major McLaughlin died in 1944, and the Blackhawks were bought by James E. Norris, who already owned the Detroit Red Wings. The Norris family practically ignored Chicago until James died in 1952 and his son James D. Norris took over the Blackhawks with his partner Arthur Wirtz. The Wirtz family still owns the Blackhawks to this day.

Stan Mikita spent his entire 22-year career in the NHL with Chicago from 1958 until 1980.

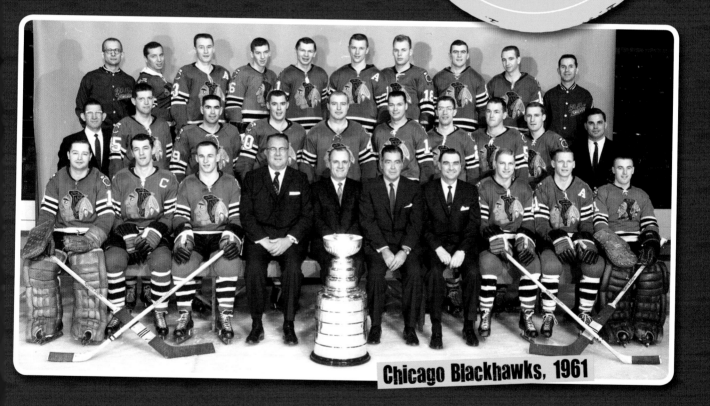

Chicago Blackhawks, 1961

Building Years

Norris and Wirtz brought Tommy Ivan from Detroit to be Chicago's new general manager in 1954, and he began to build the team back to respectability. Chicago won the Stanley Cup again in 1961. With Bobby Hull and Stan Mikita leading the way, the Blackhawks were the NHL's most dangerous scoring team for the rest of the 1960s.

THE STANLEY CUP

Cup Facts

First Awarded: 1893

Brainchild: Frederick Arthur Stanley, aka Lord Stanley of Preston, aka 6th **governor general** of Canada, aka **Queen Victoria**'s representative in Canada, aka a keen hockey fan, later also known as the 16th Earl of Derby (a noble in the United Kingdom).

Why: As an award to Canada's best amateur hockey club. By 1908, professional teams competed for it, and by 1929, only NHL teams.

Where: The cup has traveled the world, but has a permanent home at the Hockey Hall of Fame in Toronto, Canada.

Cup Stats

Height: 35.25 inches (89.5 cm)
Weight: 34.5 pounds (15.6 kg)

Chicago's Louis Trudel had his last name misspelled as TRUDELL on the Stanley Cup in 1938. Pete Palangio's name appears twice that year, once correctly and once as PALAGIO.

Cup Terms and Nicknames

Holy Grail of Hockey
A **metaphor** for the cup's status as an almost sacred relic of hockey.

Lord Stanley's Mug
A name that acknowledges the original donor while gently poking fun at the cup's purpose. In NHL cup-winning tradition, the winning team often drinks from the cup.

Challenge Cup
The decorative punch bowl bought by Lord Stanley from a silversmith in London, U.K., for 10 guineas (roughly $50) and engraved with the words "Dominion Hockey Challenge Cup." It also refers to the original era of cup competition (1893–1913).

Presentation Cup
The cup that is presented to teams on the ice includes a duplicate of the original bowl created in 1963 when the cup was becoming too weak.

Replica Cup
The Stanley Cup made in 1993 for use as a stand-in at the Hockey Hall of Fame.

Stovepipe Cup
As new bands of silver were added to the cup to accommodate the many engraved names, the cup began to look like the exhaust pipe of an old-fashioned wood stove. The term stovepipe cup describes the growing cup.

Chicago's Winning Years

1934 over Detroit Red Wings
1938 over Toronto Maple Leafs
1961 over Detroit Red Wings
2010 over Philadelphia Flyers
2013 over Boston Bruins
2015 over Tampa Bay Lightning

Cup and a Medal

Jonathan Toews, Duncan Keith, and Brent Seabrook

won **Olympic gold medals** with Team Canada and the **Stanley Cup** with Chicago in 2010.

Chicago Stanleys by the Numbers

15 teams in NHL history have reached the Stanley Cup Finals after finishing the regular season with more losses than wins. Only two have won it. Chicago (14–25–9) in 1937–38 and Toronto (22–25–13) in 1948–49.

17 players in NHL history have scored the Stanley Cup-winning goal in overtime. Mush March did it for Chicago in 1934 and Patrick Kane did it in 2010. Toe Blake scored for Montreal to beat Chicago in 1944.

Third Time Lucky

3 Marian Hossa was a member of the Pittsburgh Penguins in 2008 when they lost the Stanley Cup Finals to Detroit. In 2009, he played for Detroit when they lost the cup to Pittsburgh. In 2010, Hossa won the cup with Chicago. He's the only player in hockey history to play for the cup with three different teams in three straight seasons.

> "I have for some time been thinking that it would be a good thing if there were a challenge cup which should be held from year to year by the champion hockey team in the Dominion (of Canada)."
>
> — Lord Stanley, 1892

Stan for Stanley

Chicago general manager Stan Bowman was named after the Stanley Cup, which his father Scotty Bowman won as coach of the Montreal Canadiens a month before Stan was born in 1973.

> "Once you win the cup once, you feel like it's yours. You don't want to give it up."
>
> — Jonathan Toews after Chicago's 2013 Stanley Cup win

Put the Cup Down, Sir!

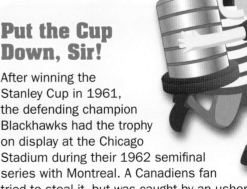

After winning the Stanley Cup in 1961, the defending champion Blackhawks had the trophy on display at the Chicago Stadium during their 1962 semifinal series with Montreal. A Canadiens fan tried to steal it, but was caught by an usher and a policeman. He had to spend a night in jail and was fined $10.

BLACKHAWKS' BEST

Bobby Hull and Stan Mikita both broke in with the Blackhawks in the 1950s, and both rewrote the NHL record book in the 1960s. They are still the two biggest stars in Chicago hockey history.

The Golden Jet

Bobby Hull was the youngest player in the NHL when he began his career as an 18-year-old in 1957–58. By the time he was 21, he was the best scorer in the game. Hull became just the third player in NHL history to score 50 goals in a season in 1961–62. He set a new record with 54 goals in 1965–66, and broke that with 58 goals in 1968–69. By his last season in Chicago in 1971–72, Hull had scored at least 50 goals five times when only one other player (Boston's Phil Esposito) had managed it even twice. Hull won the Art Ross Trophy as the NHL scoring leader three times, and the Hart Trophy as MVP twice. With his blazing speed, his booming slap shot, and his blond good looks, Bobby Hull was known as "The Golden Jet." There was no Rocket Richard Trophy in his era, but Hull led the NHL in goals seven times in his career. That's an NHL record no one has been able to match. In 1965–66, Hull also set an NHL record of 97 points in one season.

Bobby Hull

Stan the Man

Stan Mikita scored plenty of goals, but he was even better at setting up his teammates. He led the NHL in assists for three straight seasons in the mid, 1960s, setting a new league record with 59 assists in 1964–65 then breaking it with 62 assists in 1966–67. That year, he also tied teammate Bobby Hull's NHL record of 97 points in one season, which Hull had set the previous season. Mikita led the NHL in scoring four times in his career. He was the first player ever to win three major awards in one season when he won the Art Ross (scoring leader), Hart (MVP) and Lady Byng (sportsmanship) trophies in 1966–67. Then he won them all again in 1967–68.

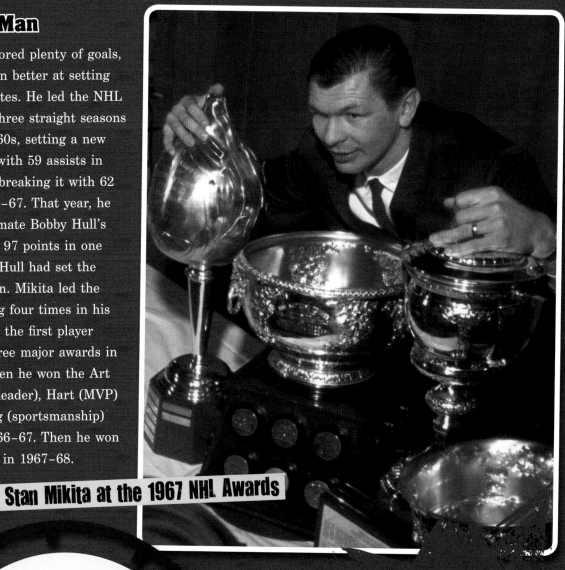

Stan Mikita at the 1967 NHL Awards

120

Although it was impossible to get an accurate reading in his day, it was said that **Bobby Hull's slap shot** reached **120 miles per hour (193 kph)**!

Bobby Hull was the third player in NHL history to score 500 career goals, and the second to score 600. His son Brett Hull is one of seven players in NHL history to top 700 goals.

GREAT GOALIES

Over the years, Chicago has had dozens of goalies. That means a number of top-notch net minders have played in the Blackhawks' crease. Some started out playing with other NHL teams, but spent the best years of their career in the **Windy City**.

Charlie Gardiner

Charlie Gardiner (who is sometimes known as Chuck Gardiner) joined the Blackhawks for their second season of 1927–28. During his first two years, Gardiner was the best player on a very bad team. People praised him for his fine play, and they also loved his great attitude. He could often be heard shouting encouragement to his teammates or joking with the fans in the stands. Soon, Gardiner was the best goalie in the NHL, winning the Vezina Trophy in 1931–32 and 1933–34. He also led Chicago to its first Stanley Cup championship in 1934. Gardiner had been sick for much of the season with badly **infected** tonsils. He never got treatment and the infection spread. Sadly, Gardiner died that summer. He was only 29 years old.

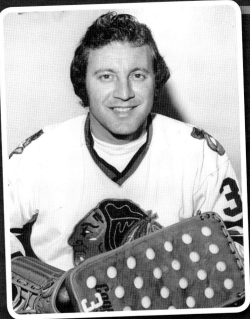

Tony Esposito

While his brother Phil became the top scorer in hockey with Boston during the early 1970s, Tony Esposito became one of the top goalies with Chicago. Tony had played briefly for Montreal in 1968–69, but he was still considered a rookie when the Blackhawks acquired him before the 1969–70 season. His first year with Chicago was one for the ages. Esposito led the NHL with 38 wins, but it was his 15 shutouts that were so spectacular. No one had posted that many shutouts since the 1928–29 season. No one has matched Esposito's total since. Esposito won both the Vezina Trophy as best goalie and the Calder Trophy as Rookie of the Year that season. He'd go on to win the Vezina Trophy two more times.

Ed Belfour

It was a long climb to the NHL for Ed Belfour. He spent three seasons in junior hockey, a year playing university hockey, and two years in the minors before he finally got a chance with Chicago in 1990–91. Belfour made up for lost time with a brilliant rookie season. He led the NHL with 43 wins and a 2.47 goals-against average. Like Tony Esposito, he won the Vezina and the Calder trophies. A year later, Belfour led Chicago to the Stanley Cup Finals, but they lost to Pittsburgh.

Glenn Hall shared the 1966-67 Vezina Trophy with teammate Denis DeJordy.

Glenn Hall

Glenn Hall joined Chicago in 1957–58 after spending two years with Detroit. Over the next few years, Hall set a remarkable record for goalies by playing 502 games in a row. When playoff games are added, Hall played 552 straight games over more than seven seasons. Hall won the Vezina twice with the Blackhawks and once with the St. Louis Blues.

BLACKHAWKS BY THE NUMBERS

5 Goals
in one game by Grant Mulvey to set a Blackhawks record in a 9-5 win over St. Louis on February 3, 1982.

6 Assists
in one game by Pat Stapleton to set a team record in a 9–5 win over Detroit on March 30, 1969.

7 Points
in one game (four goals, three assists) by Max Bentley in a 10-1 win over the New York Rangers on January 28, 1943. Grant Mulvey tied the team record when he added two assists during his five-goal game.

Hats Off!

Bill Mosienko scored the **NHL's fastest hat trick** on **March 23, 1952**. The three goals came within 21 seconds in the third period for a 7-6 Blackhawks win over the New York Rangers.
Times: 6:09 6:20 6:30

The Blackhawks set single-season team records with **52 wins** and **112 points** in 2009–10.

Chicago set a team record by scoring **12 goals** in a game in a **12-0 win** over Philadelphia on January 30, 1969.

Blackhawks Regular-Season Franchise Leaders (Career)

Games	Goals	Assists	Points	Wins	Shutouts	Goals-Against Average
1,394	604	926	1,467	413	74	2.02
Stan Mikita	Bobby Hull	Stan Mikita	Stan Mikita	Tony Esposito	Tony Esposito	Charlie Gardiner

Hanging in the Rafters

Teams retire jerseys when a player has a career-ending injury or they are just plain awesome. The following numbers have all been retired by the Chicago Blackhawks.

Glenn Hall (1957–67)	Pierre Pilote (1955–68)	Keith Magnuson (1969–80)	Bobby Hull (1957–72)	Denis Savard (1980–90, 1995–97)	Stan Mikita (1958–80)	Tony Esposito (1969–84)
1	**3**	**3**	**9**	**18**	**21**	**35**

The Blackhawks have **given up 12 goals** in a game five times, including in a 12-9 loss to Edmonton on December 11, 1985. The total of 21 goals in that game tied an NHL record first set on January 10, 1920, when the Montreal Canadiens beat the Toronto St. Patricks 14-7.

Blackhawks Franchise Leaders (Season)

Goals	Assists	Points	Wins	Shutouts	Goals-Against Average
58	**87**	**131**	**43**	**15**	**1.63**
Bobby Hull	Denis Savard	Denis Savard	Ed Belfour	Tony Esposito	Charlie Gardiner
(1968–69)	(1981–82, 1987–88)	(1987–88)	(1990–91)	(1969–70)	(1933–34)

BLACK, WHITE, AND RED

The Blackhawks have used an American Indian warrior head as their logo since the team's beginning. It is an iconic sports symbol. It's also one that has become controversial.

Behind the Name

Fred McLaughlin chose the name "Blackhawks" for his team to honor his own military heritage, but where did his U.S. infantry division get its name? Black Hawk (1767–1838) was the name of a leader and warrior of the Sauk people. His actual name was Ma-ka-tai-me-she-kia-kiak. Black Hawk fought with the British against the Americans during the War of 1812. In 1832, he led Sauk and allied warriors in a conflict named after him: the Black Hawk War. He wanted to prevent his people from losing their lands to American settlers, and he became a symbol of Native American resistance.

Chief Black Hawk

Chicago has mainly worn either a red sweater with a few black and white stripes, or a white sweater with a few black and red stripes. Sometimes the team has worn a mainly black sweater with a few red and white stripes. No matter what the main color, the team's sweaters have also featured a letter C (usually in yellow) with crossed tomahawks on the arms since 1955.

In 2014, a panel of seven experts assembled by *The Hockey News* ranked the Blackhawks logo as #1 in the NHL.

Warrior Logo

Right from their first season in 1926–27, the Chicago Blackhawks used a simple drawing of a Native American warrior head for their logo. The logo and the team's first uniforms were designed by Major McLaughlin's wife Irene Castle. In 1927–28, the Blackhawks reversed their colors to be mainly black with white stripes. Some red was added in 1934–35, and some color was added to the logo too that year, too. A more realistic warrior head logo was first used in 1937–38, when the uniforms were redesigned to feature multiple black, red, and white stripes. Another redesign of the uniform came in 1955–56. The logo has changed a bit since then, but that was the season the team introduced the basic look that Chicago still wears to this day. Some sports teams and fans are starting to acknowledge that using team names, logos, and mascots based on people or symbols from other cultures is wrong because they **misrepresent** the culture. The logos are often **stereotypes** or cartoon-like. So far, the Blackhawks have no plans to change their logo, but it may happen in the future.

Black Hawks logo 1937–55

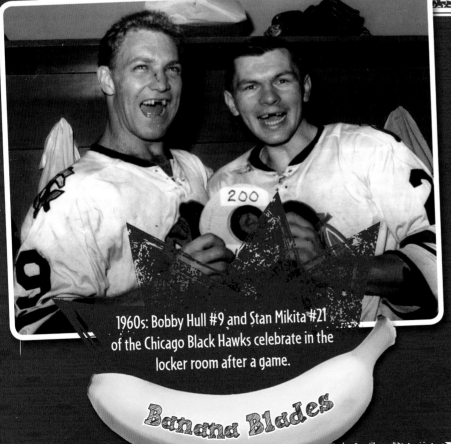

1960s: Bobby Hull #9 and Stan Mikita #21 of the Chicago Black Hawks celebrate in the locker room after a game.

Banana Blades

On the Curve

They probably didn't actually invent them, but Stan Mikita and Bobby Hull popularized the use of curved blades on hockey sticks during the 1960s. They discovered that curving the blades of their sticks made their shots faster and harder, and also caused the puck to dart unpredictably. Mikita and Hull used such big curves they became known as "Banana Blades." Soon the NHL had to pass new rules to limit the amount that blades could be curved.

TROPHY WINNERS

The Stanley Cup is the hockey prize all teams want to win the most, but here's a look at some of the Blackhawks players who've won the NHL's top individual trophies.

All-American Trophy Haul

Patrick Kane became the first American-born player to win the Art Ross Trophy when he led the NHL in scoring in 2015–16. The trophy is awarded to the league leader in regular season points. Kane was also the first player born and raised in the United States to win the Hart Trophy as NHL MVP that season.

Chicago First

Roy Conacher was the first Chicago player to win the Art Ross Trophy in 1948-49.

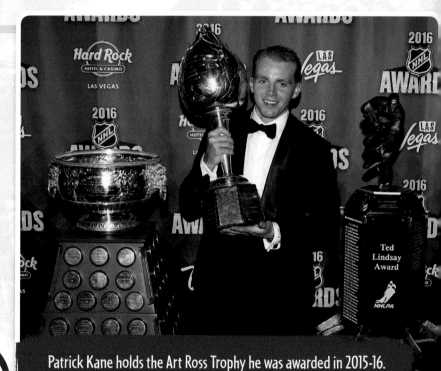

Patrick Kane holds the Art Ross Trophy he was awarded in 2015-16. He also won the Hart Trophy, as well as the Ted Lindsay Award as most outstanding player from the NHL Players' Association.

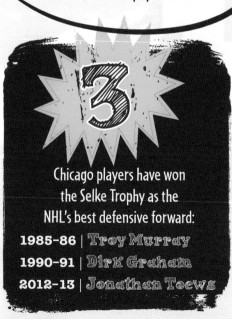

3

Chicago players have won the Selke Trophy as the NHL's best defensive forward:

1985-86 | Troy Murray
1990-91 | Dirk Graham
2012-13 | Jonathan Toews

Chicago's Hart Trophy Winners

1945-46 | Max Bentley
1953-54 | Al Rollins
1964-65 | Bobby Hull
1965-66 | Bobby Hull
1966-67 | Stan Mikita
1967-68 | Stan Mikita
2015-16 | Patrick Kane

The Hull and Mikita Show

Art Ross Trophy wins for two Chicago players in nine seasons from 1959 to 1968:

1959-60 | Bobby Hull
1961-62 | Bobby Hull
1963-64 | Stan Mikita
1964-65 | Stan Mikita
1965-66 | Bobby Hull
1966-67 | Stan Mikita
1967-68 | Stan Mikita

From left to right, the Frank J. Selke Trophy, Presidents' Trophy, Clarence Campbell Bowl, Stanley Cup, Conn Smythe Trophy and William M. Jennings Trophy sit in the Chicago Blackhawks dressing room.

Bentley Bros

Doug Bentley led the NHL in scoring with Chicago in 1942-43. His brother and Blackhawks teammate Max Bentley was the scoring leader in 1945-46 and 1946-47. At that time, there was not yet a trophy for the NHL's top scorer.

Winning Rookies

The Calder Trophy is named after the NHL's first president, Frank Calder, who held the position for 26 years (1917–43). It was his idea to present a trophy to the league's top rookie. After he died, the NHL named the trophy after him. Chicago's Calder winners are:

1935-36	Mike Karakas
1937-38	Cully Dahlstrom
1954-55	Ed Litzenberger
1959-60	Bill Hay
1969-70	Tony Esposito
1982-83	Steve Larmer
1990-91	Ed Belfour
2007-08	Patrick Kane
2015-16	Artemi Panarin

ROOKIE

4 Chicago defensemen have combined to win the Norris Trophy eight times

1962-63	Pierre Pilote
1963-64	Pierre Pilote
1964-65	Pierre Pilote
1981-82	Doug Wilson
1992-93	Chris Chelios
1995-96	Chris Chelios
2009-10	Duncan Keith
2013-14	Duncan Keith

BEHIND THE BENCH

Major McLaughlin fired coaches like crazy in Chicago's early years. Few lasted even one full season. Over the years, some Blackhawks coaches have managed to hang on longer and a few have spent their entire career with the Blackhawks.

Coach Q

Joel Quenneville was named head coach of the Chicago Blackhawks on October 16, 2008. Before that, he'd been the coach of the Colorado Avalanche and of the St. Louis Blues. Before that, Quenneville spent 13 seasons as an NHL defenseman with five different teams. He and Jacques Lemaire are the only men in hockey history to play at least 800 games in the NHL and coach at least 1,000 games. Quenneville played his last NHL season in 1990–91 and became an NHL coach in 1996–97. Entering the 2017–18 season, Quenneville has coached 1,539 regular-season games and has a record of 851–487–201 over 21 seasons. He ranks second all-time in coaching victories behind NHL leader Scotty Bowman, who won 1,244 games in 30 seasons. In the playoffs, Quenneville has coached Chicago to the Stanley Cup in 2010, 2013, and 2015.

Joel Quenneville hoists the Stanley Cup at the Blackhawks' 2015 Championship Rally.

Blackhawks Coaching Leaders

	Seasons	Games	Record	Stanley Cups
Billy Reay	1963–76	1,012	516–335–161	0
Joel Quenneville*	2008–Present	700	413–204–83	3
Bob Pulford	1977–79, 1982, 1985–87, 2000	433	186–179–68	0
Rudy Pilous	1958–63	387	162–151–74	1
Mike Keenan	1988–92	320	153–126–41	0

* still active

Just Call Him Tommy

Tommy Gorman became coach of the Blackhawks midway through the 1932–33 season. At the time, he was the tenth man to coach Chicago in just seven seasons! Gorman led Chicago to the Stanley Cup in 1933–34, but resigned after the season. He was later hired by the Montreal Maroons and led them to the Stanley Cup in 1934–35. Gorman is the only coach in NHL history to lead two different teams to the Stanley Cup in back-to-back seasons.

Brother Coach

Viking, Alberta-born brothers Darryl and Brian Sutter both coached the Blackhawks—although not at the same time. The brothers are two of six Sutters (there are seven altogether) who played in the NHL. Darryl spent his entire playing career with the Blackhawks, then went on to be assistant coach and coach of the team from 1979 to 1987. Brian played for the St. Louis Blues and later coached for Chicago 2001 to 2004. In fact, of the six NHL-playing Sutters, only one did not play or coach for Chicago at some point in their career.

Alpo Suhonen of Finland and Ivan Hlinka of the Czech Republic were the first two men born and raised in Europe to coach an NHL team. Suhonen lasted just one season with the Blackhawks in 2000–01. Hlinka spent two seasons with Pittsburgh.

BLACKHAWKS BITS AND PIECES

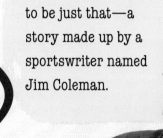

Crazy Eights

8 straight games without a goal for Chicago during the 1928–29 season. That's an NHL record for futility that's not likely to be matched! Chicago scored just 33 goals during the entire 44-game season.

28 consecutive seasons in the playoffs from 1970 to 1998. Only Boston, with 29 straight seasons from 1967 to 1996, has enjoyed a longer streak.

28 hat tricks by Bobby Hull is a Blackhawks record. Hull had 24 games with three goals and four games when he scored four goals.

A Bit of Afternoon Hockey?
The first afternoon game in NHL history was played in Chicago on March 19, 1933. The Blackhawks beat the Detroit Red Wings 4-3.

Happy Birthday!

Blackhawk Patrick Sharp scored three goals in a 7-2 win over Colorado on December 27, 2013, to become the first Chicago player ever to score a hat trick on his birthday. Sharp turned 32 that day.

Hex or Hoax?

Major McLaughlin fired coach Pete Muldoon after Chicago's first season in 1926–27. According to legend, Muldoon warned him: "Fire me, Major, and you'll never finish first. I'll put a curse on this team that will hoodoo it until the end of time." It took until 1966–67 before Chicago ever finished the regular-season in first place. Muldoon's curse is a great Blackhawks story, but it is believed to be just that—a story made up by a sportswriter named Jim Coleman.

500- Goal Club

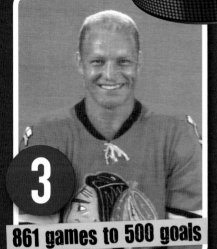

3

861 games to 500 goals

Bobby Hull became the 3rd player in NHL history to hit that milestone on February 21, 1970.

2

1,045 games to 500 goals

Mr. Hockey, Gordie Howe was the second player to reach the 500-goal mark in 1962.

1

863 games to 500 goals

Maurice "Rocket" Richard was the first player to score a record 500 goals in 1957.

Stan Mikita became the eighth player in NHL history to score 500 goals on February 27, 1977. It took him 1,221 games.

Double the Fun

Brothers Max and Doug Bentley both scored a hat trick in the same game when the Blackhawks beat the New York Rangers 9-7 on February 26, 1947. A third Bentley brother, Reg, played 11 games for the Blackhawks in 1942–43. Max and Doug got assists on Reg's only career goal on January 3, 1943.

Sorry, Bro

The first NHL player to score a goal against his brother was Chicago's Paul Thompson when he beat Boston's Tiny Thompson in a game on December 21, 1937. Phil Esposito of the Bruins scored two goals against his brother Tony during Tony's NHL debut on December 5, 1968. Tony was a member of the Montreal Canadiens at the time.

Zeros All Around

The Blackhawks and Maple Leafs played a game in Chicago on February 20, 1944, that ended in a 0-0 tie. There were no shootouts back then and the game featured no penalties for either team.

 goals in one period is an NHL record shared by 11 players.

Four of those players did it as members of the Blackhawks:
Max Bentley (January 28, 1943), **Clint Smith** (March 4, 1945), **Grant Mulvey** (February 3, 1982), and **Al Secord** (January 7, 1987).

TEAM RIVALRIES

Games between "Original Six" teams still have a special meaning for many hockey fans. They bring back memories of the early years of the NHL. Chicago has had a long rivalry with the Detroit Red Wings, who is another "Original Six" team. The Blackhawks have other rock-em sock-em rivals, too.

Detroit Battle Royale

Both Chicago and Detroit entered the NHL in 1926–27. Throughout their history, the Chicago Blackhawks have played more games against the Detroit Red Wings than any other team. Over the years, the two teams were often in the same division. That meant a lot of regular-season games against each other, and plenty of playoff match-ups too. Overall, Detroit has won a lot more games against Chicago during the regular season, but Chicago has a slight advantage in the playoffs. The Blackhawks have beaten the Red Wings 9 times and lost 7 times in their 16 playoff series. Chicago won its first Stanley Cup title against Detroit in 1934, and beat them the only other time they met in the Finals in 1961. Since the 2013–14 season, the Blackhawks have been in the Western Conference and Detroit has been in the East. That means they've played a lot fewer games against each other in recent years.

St. Louis Blues

No matter how the NHL has been **re-aligned** over the years, Chicago and the St. Louis Blues have played together in the same division since the 1970–71 season. The two cities are only 300 miles apart, and the long baseball rivalry between the Chicago Cubs and the St. Louis Cardinals means the fans in both cities don't like each other very much. This rivalry was at its fiercest between 1980 and 1993 when the two teams met in the playoffs eight times in 14 seasons. Games between the Blackhawks and Blues were pretty rough in those days!

Newer Kid on the Block

From 2008 until 2013, the rivalry between Chicago and the Vancouver Canucks was one of the best in hockey. They were among the two best teams in the Western Conference in those years and they met in the playoffs in 2009, 2010, and 2011. The Blackhawks won in 2009, and beat the Canucks again in 2010 when they went on to win the Stanley Cup for the first time in 49 years. When they met again in 2011, Vancouver won the first three games, but Chicago bounced back to tie the series before the Canucks recovered to win Game 7 in overtime.

FAN FRENZY

The United Center where the Blackhawks play is known as "The Madhouse on Madison." The name began with the team's old arena, the Chicago Stadium, which had a reputation as the NHL's noisiest arena.

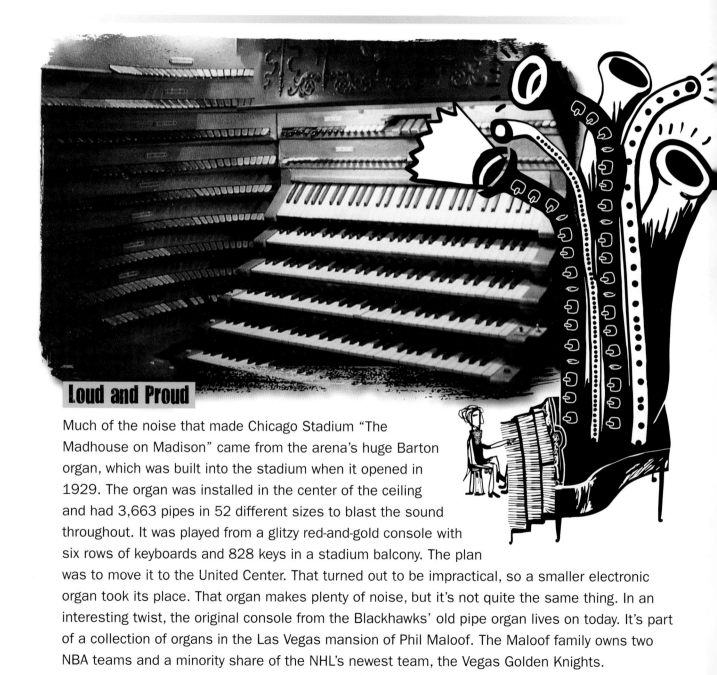

Loud and Proud

Much of the noise that made Chicago Stadium "The Madhouse on Madison" came from the arena's huge Barton organ, which was built into the stadium when it opened in 1929. The organ was installed in the center of the ceiling and had 3,663 pipes in 52 different sizes to blast the sound throughout. It was played from a glitzy red-and-gold console with six rows of keyboards and 828 keys in a stadium balcony. The plan was to move it to the United Center. That turned out to be impractical, so a smaller electronic organ took its place. That organ makes plenty of noise, but it's not quite the same thing. In an interesting twist, the original console from the Blackhawks' old pipe organ lives on today. It's part of a collection of organs in the Las Vegas mansion of Phil Maloof. The Maloof family owns two NBA teams and a minority share of the NHL's newest team, the Vegas Golden Knights.

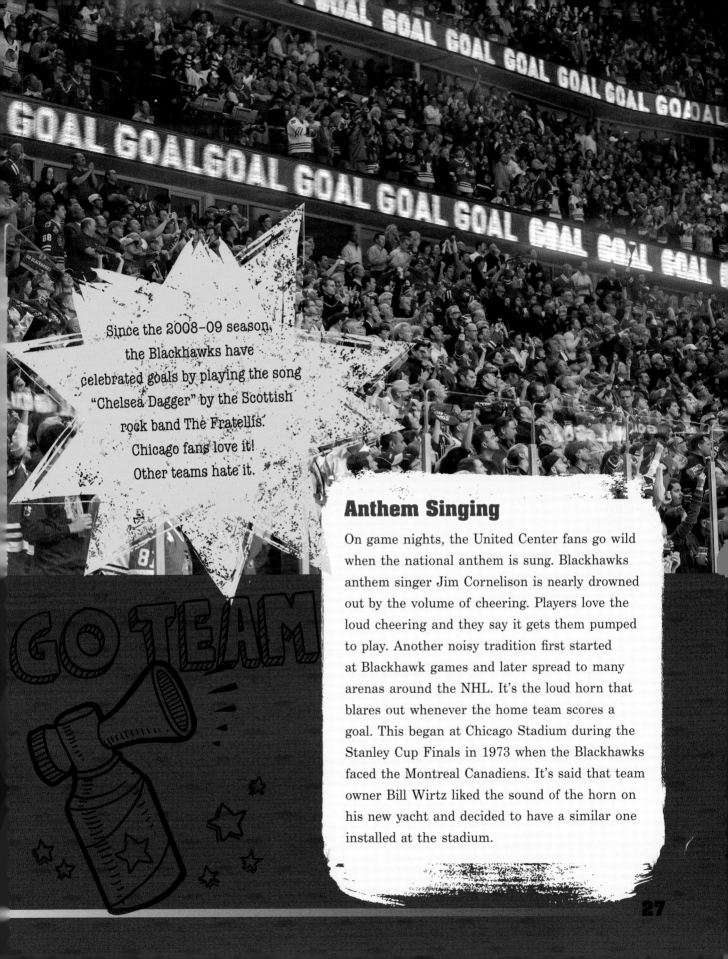

Since the 2008–09 season, the Blackhawks have celebrated goals by playing the song "Chelsea Dagger" by the Scottish rock band The Fratellis. Chicago fans love it! Other teams hate it.

Anthem Singing

On game nights, the United Center fans go wild when the national anthem is sung. Blackhawks anthem singer Jim Cornelison is nearly drowned out by the volume of cheering. Players love the loud cheering and they say it gets them pumped to play. Another noisy tradition first started at Blackhawk games and later spread to many arenas around the NHL. It's the loud horn that blares out whenever the home team scores a goal. This began at Chicago Stadium during the Stanley Cup Finals in 1973 when the Blackhawks faced the Montreal Canadiens. It's said that team owner Bill Wirtz liked the sound of the horn on his new yacht and decided to have a similar one installed at the stadium.

ON HOME ICE

To the Ancient Romans, the Colosseum was a massive entertainment venue where circuses, chariot races, and gladiator battles were held. The Chicago Coliseum, and later the Stadium were also home to the Barnum and Bailey Circus, roller derby, political party "races," and epic hockey matches and fights.

Chicago Coliseum

First Blackhawks game: November 17, 1926. They beat the Toronto St. Patricks 4-1.

Seating capacity: 6,000.

Hawks home ice: 1928–29 season and into the start of the 1929–30 season. The team also played its first three home games there in 1932–33.

Chicago Stadium

- **Opened:** with a boxing match on March 28, 1929.
- **First Blackhawks game:** A 3–1 victory over the Pittsburgh Pirates on December 15, 1929.
- **Cost of construction:** $9.5 million. That would be equivalent to about $133 million today.
- **Official capacity for hockey:** 17,317 seats, and 18,472 including standing room.
- **Largest crowd ever for a hockey game:** 20,069 on April 10, 1982 against the Minnesota North Stars.
- **Final game:** April 28, 1994. Chicago lost 1–0 to the Toronto Maple Leafs.
- **Honorable mentions:** Home of the Chicago Bulls of the National Basketball Association (NBA) from 1967 to 1994. The Chicago Bears of the National Football League played an exhibition game in the Stadium in 1930 and an NFL playoffs game in 1932.
- **Swan song:** Torn down in 1995 and is currently a parking lot for the United Center.

United Center

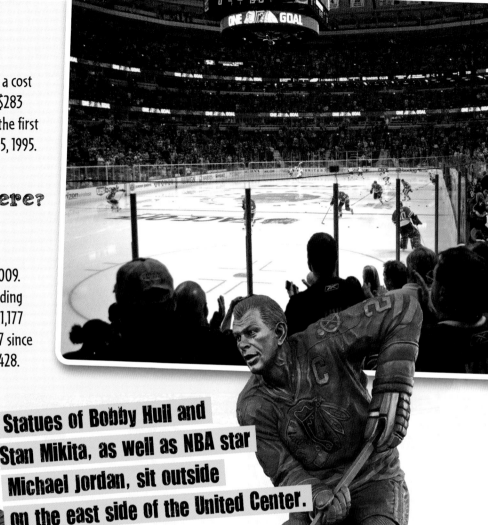

Built: Between 1992 and 1994 at a cost of $175 million, which would be about $283 million today. Due to an NHL lockout, the first Blackhawks home game was January 25, 1995. Chicago beat Edmonton 5–1.

Who else lives there?
Home to the Chicago Bulls

Seating capacity:
For hockey was 20,500 from 1995 to 2009. It has been 19,717 since then, with standing room of 23,129. For basketball, it was 21,177 from 1995 to 2009 and has been 20,917 since then. With standing room, it holds 22,428. Capacity for concerts is 23,500.

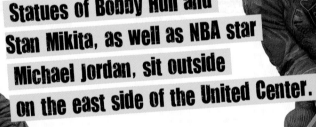

Statues of Bobby Hull and Stan Mikita, as well as NBA star Michael Jordan, sit outside on the east side of the United Center.

MIKITA
AWKS

9
ACHIEVEMENTS

21
ACHIEVEMEN

FIRST PLAYER IN NHL HISTORY TO WIN
LADY BYNG TROPHIES IN SAME Y

Glossary

dynasty A family of rulers, a team owned by a family, or a team that has won championships year after year

free agency A player who does not have a contract with a specific team and can receive offers to play from many teams

governor general Canada's head of state, who represents the queen or king

infected Having a disease caused by germs

metaphor A word or phrase that is used to refer to something else to show similarities

misrepresent To describe something in a false or misleading way

Queen Victoria The queen of the United Kingdom from 1837-1901; at the time Lord Stanley was governor general of Canada

re-aligned Put together in a new way

stereotypes Unfair and often untrue beliefs people have about others

Windy City A nickname for Chicago because of the strong lake winds that rip through the city, especially in fall and winter

Further Reading

If you're a fan of the Chicago Blackhawks, you may enjoy these books:

The Home Team: Chicago Blackhawks by Holly Preston. Always Books Ltd., 2015.

The Big Book of Hockey for Kids by Eric Zweig. Scholastic Canada, 2017.

The Ultimate Book of Hockey Trivia for Kids by Eric Zweig. Scholastic Canada, 2015.

The Screech Owls series by Roy MacGregor.

Websites to Check Out

Official Hockey Hall of Fame: **www.hhof.com**

Hockey Canada: **www.hockeycanada.ca/multimedia/kids/**

Official National Hockey League's official website: **www.nhl.com**

Official Chicago Blackhawks website: **www.nhl.com/blackhawks**

Test Your Blackhawks' Knowledge

1. Which Blackhawks player set the NHL hat trick record with three goals in 21 seconds?

a) Chris Chelios
b) Bill Mosienko
c) Stan Mikita
d) Jonathan Toews

2. Which Chicago superstar scored 50 goals or more five times for the Blackhawks?

a) Stan Mikita
b) Tony Amonte
c) Bobby Hull
d) Eric Nesterenko

3. Which of these was not a Bentley brother who played for the Blackhawks?

a) Doug
b) Jack
c) Max
d) Reg

4. Which of these Blackhawks stars was the #1 NHL draft pick in 2007?

a) Patrick Kane
b) Duncan Keith
c) Brent Seabrook
d) Jonathan Toews

5. Which two trophies did Tony Esposito and Ed Belfour both win during their first seasons with Chicago?

a) The Vezina Trophy and the Calder Trophy
b) The Selke Trophy and the Calder Trophy
c) The Hart Trophy and the Conn Smyth Trophy
d) The Calder Trophy and the Lady Byng Memorial Trophy

1. b) Bill Mosienko; 2. c) Bobby Hull; 3. b) Jack; 4. a) Patrick Kane; 5. a) The Vezina Trophy and the Calder Trophy

Places to Go

If you're ever in Toronto, be sure to visit the Hockey Hall of Fame. If you're in Chicago, you can see a game at the United Center. Even if you don't have tickets, you can take a picture with the statues of Bobby Hull and Stan Mikita, or basketball legend Michael Jordan. Depending on the season, there's baseball, football, and soccer games in other parts of the city, too.

About the Author

By the age of ten, Eric Zweig was already a budding sports fanatic who was filling his school news books with game reports instead of current events. He has been writing professionally about sports and sports history since 1985. Eric has written many sports books for adults and children, including the novels *Hockey Night in the Dominion of Canada* (Lester Publishing, 1992) and *Fever Season* (Dundurn Press, 2009). Eric is a member of the Society for International Hockey Research and the Society for American Baseball Research. Visit Eric's web site at ericzweig.com

Index

American players 6
anthem 27
Art Ross Trophy 10, 11, 18
assists 11, 14, 15

Belfour, Ed 13, 15, 19
Bentley, Doug 19, 23
Bentley, Max 14, 18, 19, 23
Bentley, Reg 23
Black Hawk, Chief 16
Black Hawks to Blackhawks 6
Blake, Toe 9
Bowman, Scotty 9, 20
Bowman, Stan 9

Calder Trophy 4, 5, 13, 19
Castle, Irene 17
"Chelsea Dagger" song 27
Chicago Coliseum 28
Chicago Stadium 9, 26–27
Clarence Campbell Trophy 19
coaches 6, 20–21, 22
Conacher, Roy 18
Conn Smythe Trophy 19
Cornelison, Jim 27
curse 22
curved sticks 17

defensive forwards 18
Detroit Red Wings 5, 7, 8, 9, 22, 24
dynasty 5

Esposito, Phil 10, 13, 23
Esposito, Tony 13, 14, 15, 19, 23
Evans, Jack 5

first game 28

Gardiner, Charlie 12, 14, 15
general managers 7, 9
goalies 12–13
Gorman, Tommy 21

Hall, Glenn 13, 15
Hart Trophy 10, 11, 18
hat tricks 14, 22, 23
horn 27
Hossa, Marian 5, 9
Howe, Gordie 23
Hull, Bobby "The Golden Jet" 5, 7, 10, 11, 14, 15, 17, 18, 23, 29
Hull, Brett 11

Ivan, Tommy 7

jersey colors 16, 17
jerseys, retired 15

Kane, Patrick 4, 5, 18, 19
Keith, Duncan 5, 9, 19

Lady Byng Trophy 11
logo 16, 17

"**M**adhouse on Madison, The" 26
March, Mush 9
McLaughlin, Major Frederic 6, 7, 17, 22
Mikita, Stan 5, 7, 11, 14, 15, 17, 18, 23, 29
Montreal Canadiens 6, 9, 13, 15, 23, 27
Mosienko, Bill 14
Muldoon, Pete 22
Mulvey, Grant 14, 23
MVP awards 10, 11, 18

NHL records 11, 14, 15, 22, 23
Norris family 7
Norris, James D. 7
Norris Trophy 19

Olympic gold medals 9
organ music 26
"Original Six, The" 6, 24

Pilote, Pierre 5, 15, 19
playoffs 4, 5, 13, 20, 22, 24, 25, 28
Presidents' Trophy 19

Quenneville, Joel 20

records
  5-goal games 14
  50-goal seasons 10
  assists 11, 14, 15
  career goals 11
  coaching 20
  goals 10, 14, 15, 23
  goals-against average 13, 14, 15
  hat tricks 14, 22
  NHL 10, 11, 15, 22, 23
  player 10, 11, 13, 14, 15, 22, 23
  points 11, 14, 15
  shutouts 13, 15
  straight games 13
  straight games without goals 22
  team 14, 22
  wins 14, 15
Richard, Maurice "Rocket" 23
Rookie of the Year 4, 13

St. Louis Blues 13, 20, 21, 25
Savard, Denis 15
Seabrook, Brent 5, 9
Selke Trophy 18, 19
Sharp, Patrick 22
shutouts 13, 14, 15
Stanley Cup 8–9, 19
Stanley Cup Finals 9, 13, 24, 27
Stanley Cup wins 4, 5, 6, 7, 8, 9, 19, 20, 21, 25
Stanley, Lord 8, 9
Stapleton, Pat 14
Sutter, Brian 21
Sutter, Darryl 21

Team Canada 9
team name 6
Thompson, Paul 23
Toews, Jonathan 4, 5, 9, 18
Toronto Maple Leafs 5, 6, 8, 9, 23, 28
Toronto St. Patricks 15, 28
traditions 26–27

uniforms 16, 17
United Center 28, 29

Vancouver Canucks 25
Vezina Trophy 12, 13

William M. Jennings Trophy 19
Wirtz, Arthur 7
Wirtz family 7, 27